The *Great*

Constitution

A BOOK FOR YOUNG AMERICANS

The Great Constitution

★ ★ A BOOK FOR YOUNG AMERICANS ★ ★

by

HENRY STEELE COMMAGER

EASTERN ACORN PRESS

A LOU REDA BOOK

Contents

The Great
Constitution

A BOOK FOR YOUNG AMERICANS

I

MOST NATIONS don't have to be made. They are there already. They have always been there. No one had to *make* France or England or Denmark. You might say that history made them. They don't have any "fathers" or any "birthday."

The United States is different. Remember how Lincoln put it in the Gettysburg Address: "Our fathers *brought forth* on this continent a new nation."

This is just what they did, too: They brought it forth; they almost invented it. What had been thirteen Colonies became thirteen States, and what had been thirteen States became the United States of America.

Of course, it wasn't all that easy. After all, how does one go about *making* a nation? It isn't like making a cake, you know, or a table: Just follow the directions, and presto! there it is. No one had ever *made* a nation before. There were no directions.

Since the United States has shown the way, nation-making has become common enough. Now there is a new nation almost every day. But up until the time the Fathers "brought forth" the United States, no one had ever managed to make a nation.

When Lincoln gave his Gettysburg Address, he knew just exactly when the nation had been born. It was "four score and seven years ago"—in other words, eighty-seven years ago. As he spoke in 1863, that made the date 1776. Everyone knew that 1776 meant Independence. But did it mean a new nation? That is not so clear. We sometimes think that it did. But the Declaration of Independence itself says only that "these United Colonies are, and of right ought to be, *free and independent States.*" Thirteen free and independent States don't necessarily make a nation.

Americans found this out quickly enough. They had fought together for seven years, and had won the war for independence together—something no one really expected them to do, least of all England. And there they were, in 1783, when old Benjamin Franklin and round, bright-eyed John Adams and sedate John Jay signed the treaty of peace over in Paris.

There they were, thirteen brand-new States strung along the Atlantic coast from New Hampshire to Georgia. And each State acted as if it had won the war all by itself—not little Delaware, perhaps, or Georgia, which had no population to speak of, but certainly all the big ones. What is more, each one acted as if it were an independent nation.

There was, to be sure, a union of sorts: The Confederation it was called, and it started off by saying that "each State retains its sovereign freedom and independence." Each *State! Each* State!

During the war, wise Benjamin Franklin had said that if the Americans didn't hang together they would hang separately. Well, they had managed to hang together fairly well while the fighting went on. When the war was over, there was no longer any real danger of hanging separately. But now they didn't seem to hang together very well, either.

Along in 1785 and 1786, it began to look as if the brand-new Confederation was coming apart at the seams. The government just did not work. It could not make treaties with foreign countries. It could not collect taxes or pay debts. It could not keep peace with the Indians—or fight them either, for that matter. It couldn't even do the day by day job of government, because not enough members of Congress bothered to attend the sessions.

Worse yet, the American States were threatened from without as well as from within. England had lost the war, but she was not yet ready to give up in America. She held on to Canada and, what is more, she held on to the forts and trading posts in the Ohio country—country that belonged by rights to the United States. So much for the northern boundaries.

To the south was Spain—to the south and the west, all the way from Florida to the Mississippi, and all along the Mississippi River. We now think of Spain as a small nation, but in the eighteenth century, Spain was one of the two greatest powers in the world. The Spanish flag waved all the way from the Straits of Magellan at the tip of South America to Vancouver Island on our northwest coast.

These two great powers, Spain and England, now formed a solid line all around the United States. Both hoped that the United States would break up, and both were ready to pick up the pieces.

Then, in the winter of 1786, came more trouble. Up in Massachusetts, the farmers of the Connecticut Valley grew tired of the way things were going. They were fed up with runaway prices for the things they had to buy and low prices for the things they sold; with high taxes, and with rich men in Boston foreclosing on their mortgages and trying to take away their farms. They decided that they had had enough.

Under the leadership of a Revolutionary War veteran, Daniel Shays, they went on the warpath. These men weren't really dangerous—they just wanted what they thought were their rights. But they scared the daylights out of the proper people in Boston, and of proper Americans everywhere. Here was revolution all over again—this time against an *American* government.

Henry Knox was a bookseller who had turned general and was one of George Washington's oldest and most trusted friends. He wrote Washington about the rebellion:

> This dreadful situation has alarmed every man of principle and property in New England. They start as from a dream and ask what has been the cause of our delusion. What is to afford us security against the violence of lawless men?

Actually it wasn't all that bad: Daniel Shays and

Daniel Shays and his mob take possession of a Court House.

his followers just wanted their rights. But it was hard for Knox to see that, or Washington, for that matter. George Washington burst out: "Who besides a Tory could have foreseen, or a Briton predicted it!"

Who indeed? Clearly, something had to be done if the nation were to survive. As James Madison put it, "It is not possible that a government can last long under these circumstances."

A good many of the leading men of America had seen that for some time. Now they bestirred themselves.

Two men took the lead. Both were young and ardent, but both wise beyond their years. One was Madison of Virginia, and the other, Alexander Hamilton of New York. Each had been in the thick of the Revolution—Hamilton as a soldier, Madison as a Congressman. Each had been close to the great leaders of the war—Hamilton as an aide to Washington, and Madison as a friend and disciple of Jefferson. And both were Nationalists who had been trying for years to find some way to strengthen the government of the Confederation.

When you have a problem like that on your hands, it is hard to know where to begin. Madison started by making use of a quarrel—or at least a dispute—between Virginia and Maryland over the Potomac River. If you look at your map you will

Portrait of George Washington, by Charles Willson Peale.

see that the Potomac rises in the mountains of Virginia and Pennsylvania. On its way to the sea, it forms the boundary between Virginia and Maryland.

If you stop to think about it for a moment, you will realize that a river is not a very good boundary. You cannot really use half of a river, any more than you can use half of a horse or an automobile. No wonder Virginians and Marylanders quarreled about who controlled the river! And these two weren't the only States to have river trouble. New Jersey and New York had like troubles and so, too, New Hampshire and Vermont. (To this day, the States along the Ohio and the Mississippi and the Columbia rivers have similar problems.)

Madison, therefore, had the bright idea of getting all the States together to talk over matters of commerce and navigation. At the meeting, in the pleasant little town of Annapolis in Maryland, only five States actually turned up. This was not very many out of the thirteen, but among the five were Virginia and Pennsylvania and New York. More important, among those who went to Annapolis were Madison and Hamilton.

The meeting in Annapolis didn't get very far. After all, how could it? What could five States do by themselves? And, for that matter, what was the use of talking about trade and navigation, as if these

17

Portrait of James Madison, by Gilbert Stuart.

could be separated from all other matters of government? In the 1780's—as in the 1960's—trade was tangled up with almost everything else you can think of.

Madison and Hamilton and their friends at Annapolis managed to do just one thing, but that was the best thing they could possibly have done. They sent out a call to *all* the States to meet at a really top-level conference. We would probably call it a summit conference today. The States would discuss not just trade or navigation, but *everything* connected with government. Here is the way Hamilton put it in his letter:

> Commissioners to meet at Philadelphia on the second Monday in May next, to take into consideration the situation of the United States, to devise such further provisions as shall appear to them necessary to make the Constitution of the federal government adequate to the exigencies of the Union.

It is pretty clear what this meant. It meant that the States were to send delegates who could talk about all matters of government and, more important, who could *act*.

This was a pretty big order. Let us see how it was carried out.

II

EARLY ON THE morning of May 9, 1787, George Washington mounted his horse and started off on the long ride from Mount Vernon, on the Potomac, to Philadelphia. The trip is nothing now—it lasts only a couple of hours by train, and less than an hour by air—but Washington's journey took five days. It was not an easy trip, either. It had been a rainy spring; the rivers were high and the roads were deep in mud. But that isn't what delayed Washington.

He was delayed because everywhere he went, people wanted to entertain him. They made speeches at him and arranged celebrations and dinners in his honor. This was all pleasant enough, but it took time.

When Washington reached Chester, just across the river from Philadelphia, he was met by a number of his former war-time comrades. There was also the crack Philadelphia City Cavalry, who wanted to escort him into the city. Over the broad Schuylkill River they went, then, by ferry, and on to Philadelphia.

Flags fluttered in the breeze, cannon and muskets fired off salutes, all the church bells were ringing. As it was Sunday, no one was at work, and the streets were lined with cheering crowds. What a good beginning for the Convention!

For there was going to be a Convention, after all. It had not been absolutely certain there would be such a meeting—until it became known that General Washington would attend as a delegate from Virginia. Then, one by one, all the States fell into line. (All but little Rhode Island, which simply couldn't make up its mind and never did get around to it.) Everyone wanted to follow Washington's lead. Whatever he did was the right thing to do. Everyone knew that he was the greatest man in America, and most people were ready to swear that he was the greatest man in the world.

Cavalry escort and all, Washington clattered up

Convention at Philadelphia, 1787.

the old cobbled streets of Philadelphia to the inn kept by Mrs. House, where he planned to put up for the duration of the Convention. But that would never do, thought Robert Morris, and he made Washington come home to *his* house instead.

Mr. Morris was the leading businessman and banker of Philadelphia—perhaps of the whole country. He had managed the finances of the Revolutionary War. He was either very rich or very poor, he himself never quite knew which. He ended up in jail because he couldn't pay his debts, poor fellow. Meantime, he had a big house, with lots of servants, and he gave great parties just as if

Portrait of Robert Morris,
by Charles Willson Peale.

he were really rich.

None of that mattered to Washington. What mattered was that he and Morris were old friends and they got along famously. So it was the most natural thing in the world for Washington to accept his invitation.

Only one other man in America was as famous as Washington: that was old Dr. Benjamin Franklin of Philadelphia. He was now eighty years old, and not very well, but he was as lively as ever. While he didn't go out much himself, he liked to see his friends and to discuss everything in heaven and earth.

Old State House, Congress Hall and Town Hall, Philadelphia

The very first night he was in Philadelphia, Washington went to pay his respects to Franklin. What a meeting that must have been! And what talk: about the Revolution—Franklin had helped start it; about the Confederation—Franklin had drawn up the Articles of Confederation; about the treaty of peace that gave America independence—Franklin had been the man who got the English to accept that treaty.

Now he was President of the State of Pennsylvania, and the Pennsylvania legislature had named him as one of its delegates to the Convention, to help draw up the new Constitution. So there was that to talk about, too.

The Convention was to have met the very next day after Washington arrived, but so far it didn't look much like a convention. The Pennsylvanians were there, of course—they *lived* there—and a few of the Virginians. But no one else bothered to be on time. The reason was partly bad roads. After all, if it took five days from Mount Vernon, think how long it took to get to Philadelphia from Boston, or from Charleston, South Carolina! But the reason was partly, too, the easy-going habits of the time. People tended to let things drift, and time wasn't as important as we think it now.

It was really just as well that the others were late, for it gave Washington and Madison and their friends a chance to work out their plans. That is just what they did.

James Madison and Governor Randolph (who was related to everyone) and George Mason (a great swell who was always known as Mason of Gunston Hall), had arrived by now from Virginia. They all put up at the Indian Queen, a spacious inn just around the corner from the State House, where all the meetings were to be held.

In a few days, young Alexander Hamilton came clattering in from New York, and he put up at the Indian Queen too. After a while, the whole South

Charles Cotesworth Pinckney

Charles Pinckney

Carolina delegation—the Pinckney brothers and Governor Rutledge—were there, too. We will meet all of them later, so we don't need to bother too much with them now, just as they are getting settled.

No wonder they all wanted to put up at the Indian Queen instead of at Mrs. House's, or the City Inn, or one of the other inns. It was not only the most stylish place to stay, but it had the best food and the best service, too. When you came in, you were greeted by a Negro servant rigged out in a blue coat with red sleeves, a buff-colored vest and breeches, with a ruffled lace shirt and buckles on his shoes. Even his hair was powdered. Poor fellow—imagine being dressed like that in a hot

26

Old Indian Queen Tavern

Philadelphia summer. But he probably enjoyed it.

So many delegates to the Convention stayed at the Indian Queen that the landlord set aside a special dining room for them. Here they could have their meals in peace and—more important—could talk over their plans in private. Doubtless it was here, or perhaps in Madison's or Randolph's private rooms, that the Virginians and their friends from Pennsylvania hammered out the plan that they presented to the Convention when it finally got down to business.

During one of the many discussions of this plan, Washington—who usually had very little to say— made a remark that was to become famous. Some of the Virginians (perhaps Randolph, who was always very cautious) were saying: Let's be careful. Let's not go too fast or shock anyone with our ideas. Then Washington spoke up:

> If to please the people we offer what we ourselves disapprove, how can we afterwards defend our work? Let us raise a standard to which the wise and honest can repair. The event is in the hand of God.

That bears reading again and again. No wonder everybody remembered it, and remembers it to this day.

While the delegates waited for the others to get to Philadelphia, there was plenty to do, especially for Washington. The Society of the Cincinnati, made up of officers of the Revolutionary Army, were holding their convention in Philadelphia at the same time. Of course, Washington went to their dinners and reminisced about the war with his old comrades. There were parties almost every night, too, for all Philadelphia wanted to entertain the General, as well as the other famous delegates. Washington was kept busy just turning down invitations. He didn't turn them all down, to be sure. His Diary, really not much more than an engagement book for these weeks, is filled with notes about tea here and dinner there!

28

There were many things to see and do in this largest of American cities. There was Charles Peale's Museum, for example. It contained not only many of Peale's own paintings, but stuffed animals and birds, and skeletons of animals, and wax figures of famous Americans. There was even a figure of Peale himself, for he was famous enough.

Or there was John Bartram's Botanical Garden, just outside the city. A simple old man, Bartram, but he had been famous all over the world for his plants and flowers. What is more, he wrote so well

Bartram's house and garden.

about the birds and animals he saw on his many explorations into the wilderness, that one couldn't put his book down, it was so thrilling.

There was the University, too. The great Dr. Benjamin Rush, another of Washington's friends, presided over its medical school. He was as busy in politics as he was in medicine, ready with a new plan to cure diseases, or a new idea about teaching in the schools of the State, or a new plan for government—all at once.

Best of all, thought Washington and a good many others, was the theater. He went whenever he had a chance. It wasn't called a *theater*, as these were thought to be sinful—a waste of time and heaven knows what else. So all plays were called operas or concerts, which were supposed to be uplifting and highbrow. One night, Washington saw *The Detection; or, The Servants' Hall in an Uproar*, and on another it was Shakespeare's *Tempest*, "concluded with a Grand Masque of Neptune and Amphytrite, with Entire new Scenery, the music composed by Dr. Purcell." Did Washington enjoy that, we wonder?

For the studious and the serious-minded ones, there was always John Adams' new book on constitutions which he had finished just in time to put in the hands of members of the Convention. Madison, we know, studied it, and James Wilson of

Pennsylvania, but then, those two studied every-thing.

In a week or so, the Virginians had their plan ready. But where was the Convention? Slowly, by ones and twos, the delegates came straggling in, some on horseback, some more sedately by coach, some by sailing ship up the Delaware River to Front Street. By May 27, seven States were represented, and the leaders decided that they could go ahead with the Convention.

III

Picture then the State House, or Independence Hall as people were beginning to call it, in the very heart of the City of Brotherly Love. Better yet, you should go and see it for yourself; it is still there, just as it was when Jefferson presented his Declaration of Independence in 1776, just as it was when the Founding Fathers debated the Constitution.

Fronting on Chestnut Street, it was a handsome red brick building with a bell tower in the center, and two wings stretching to Fifth and Sixth streets.

The Reverend Manasseh Cutler, who had come down from Massachusetts to talk to the delegates about his plan for a settlement out in Ohio, was immensely impressed with the State House:

A noble building, the architecture is in a richer and grander style than any public building I have before seen. The first story is not an open walk, as is usual in buildings of this kind. In the middle is a very broad cross aisle, and a floor above supported by two rows of pillars. From this aisle is a broad opening to a large hall toward the west end, which opening is supported by arches and pillars. . . . The hall east of the aisle is employed for public business.

Behind the building was a garden, or Mall as it was called at the time, surrounded by a high brick wall. Dr. Cutler was even more impressed by the garden than by the building itself:

The Mall is small, nearly square, and does not contain more than one acre. As you enter the Mall through the State House, which is the only avenue to it, it appears to be nothing more than a large inner courtyard to the State House, ornamented with trees and walks. But

National Park Service Photo
State House Gardens, Philadelphia.

here is a fine display of rural fancy and elegance. It was so lately laid out in its present form that it has not assumed that air of grandeur which time will give it.

The trees are yet small, but most judiciously arranged. The artificial mounds of earth, and depressions, and small groves in the squares have a most delightful effect. The numerous walks are well graveled and rolled hard. They are all in a serpentine direction, which heightens the beauty and affords constant variety.

That painful sameness commonly to be met with in garden alleys, and other works of this kind, is happily avoided here, for there are no two parts of the Mall that are alike.

Too bad that across the street was the city jail, filled mostly with poor people who couldn't pay their debts. They looked out through the bars of their windows and begged passers-by for food or for money, and howled at those who didn't give them anything.

As Cutler wrote, "Whatever part of the Mall you are in, this cage of unclean birds is constantly in your view, and their doleful cries attacking your ears."

It is a good thing there was a high wall around the garden, for almost the first thing the Convention did was to vote for secrecy. They didn't want word of what they were doing to get out—and very sensible, too. They could never have spoken their minds, or made their compromises and concessions, if every word they said had been reported in the press or chewed up in the inns or over the dinner tables of Philadelphia.

So determined were the delegates to have privacy that they kept the windows of the chamber closed— imagine, in a hot Philadelphia summer! And to make sure that nobody who had no business there

Manasseh Cutler

could get in, they had sentries march up and down in front of the State House. They wanted to shut out noise as well, and they persuaded the city authorities to cover the cobblestone streets around the State House with straw. Ben Franklin probably managed that.

Portrait of Robert Morris, by Charles Willson Peale.

Here they were, then, all ready to get on with the great enterprise. The first thing was to elect a President of the Convention, and that was also the easiest. There was only one man who could even be thought of for that post of honor: George Washington, of course.

Franklin had hoped to get down to the opening meeting to nominate Washington—it would have been a nice compliment from the second greatest man in America to the greatest—but he didn't feel up to it, and instead it was Washington's host, Robert Morris, who stood up and proposed Washington as President. Everyone voted for that.

As soon as the votes were counted and the choice announced, Morris and Governor Rutledge conducted the General to the platform. Everyone noticed the chair in which he would sit: on its back was painted a picture of the sun, its rays streaming out over the horizon in all directions.

In one way, it was too bad that Washington was acting as chairman, up there on the platform. It meant that he wouldn't have any part in the debates. For, as you know, a presiding officer just presides. he doesn't talk, too. But then, Washington never was one for talking. He much preferred to listen while others did the talking.

In another way, the election of Washington as chairman that first day was the most important thing that happened in the whole Convention. It did more than anything else to make the Convention—and the Constitution—a success.

For everybody trusted George Washington—from Maine to Georgia—and they reasoned (just as you and I reason today) that if Washington was chairman, the Convention must be all right. He wouldn't be mixed up in anything that wasn't for the good of the country. He certainly wouldn't be *in charge* of something that wasn't safe and sound!

The election of Washington to the chair had one other result that was all to the good. It put the delegates on their good behavior.

Now, you might think that the behavior of the delegates was already good enough. So it was, of course: there were no scamps or scoundrels among them. But good behavior in debate and discussion is something else again. It means that a debater is not too long-winded; he lets others have their turn, and doesn't interrupt. He doesn't let his sense of humor run away with him, or his sense of self-importance, either. He is patient and courteous. He doesn't call names or make nasty comments about his fellow members or show how foolish he thinks their remarks are.

When the Convention was over, one member wrote that "scarcely a personality or offensive expression escaped during the whole session." That was, in part, Washington's doing. For with that Jove-like figure on the platform watching over all, the delegates were, of course, on their best behavior. Everybody—except maybe Franklin, or the oddly-named Daniel of St. Thomas Jenifer, who was older than Washington and had known

Gouverneur Morris

him all his life—was a little afraid of Washington.

There is a story that illustrates this—and tells us a good deal about another character as well. The other person is young Gouverneur Morris, of New York, the man who managed to talk more than any one else at the Convention. William Pierce, who painted a series of word-pictures of

40

the members of the Convention, gives us this portrait of Morris:

Mr. Gouverneur Morris is one of those geniuses in whom every species of talents combine to render him conspicuous and flourishing in public debate. He winds through all the mazes of rhetoric and throws around him such a glare that he charms, captivates and leads away the senses of all who hear him. With an infinite stretch of fancy he brings to view things when he is engaged in deep argumentation, that render all the labor of reasoning easy and pleasing.

But with all these powers he is fickle and inconstant—never pursuing one train of thinking, nor ever regular. He has gone through a very extensive course of reading, and is acquainted with all the sciences. No man has more wit—nor can anyone engage the attention more than Mr. Morris. . . .

This gentleman is about thirty-eight years old. He has been unfortunate in losing one of his legs, and getting all the flesh taken off his right arm by a scald when a youth.

But let us get back to that story. One night

41

Portrait of George Washington, by Edward Savage.

when Morris was at dinner with his companions, the talk got around to Washington, and to what an awesome person he was.

"Well, I'm not afraid of him," said Morris. When a chorus of jeers greeted this boast, Morris really became reckless. He bet the others that he would go up to Washington and slap him on the back! The next day he was more thoughtful, and should have known better. But he decided to go through with it, anyway. He didn't actually venture to slap Washington on the back—he just put his hand on Washington's arm.

"The great man turned and looked at me, and I wished the earth had yawned and swallowed me up," said Morris afterward.

One didn't take liberties with Washington!

Now everything at the State House was properly organized—Washington in the chair, ten States represented, the sentries marching up and down outside the doors, and the straw on the street. The Convention could get on with the job.

Let's look at these men as they get ready to write what turned out to be the most important Constitution in the history of the world. Imagine such a document coming from a little country off on the fringe of civilization, a country whose total population was less than that of Los Angeles or Chicago today!

The group that hammered out the Constitution was a small one, really not larger than a good-sized committee. Usually there were about thirty or thirty-five delegates present, and—as usual with any committee—about half of them did most of the talking.

Nearly all the men knew one another already, for eighteenth-century America was a small and intimate world. They had fought together in the Revolution; they had worked together in Congress; they had known one another and written letters back and forth and visited one another's homes.

Twenty-one of them had fought in the Revolution. If they had all worn their uniforms (as Washington did when he was being painted by the tireless Charles Peale), it would have been a colorful assemblage. Eight of them had signed the Declaration of Independence. Seven of them had been governors of their States. Almost all of them had served, at one time or another, in the Continental Congresses.

Yet, for all this experience, it was a young group. Two of them—the brilliant Charles Pinckney of South Carolina, and Jonathan Dayton of New Jersey—were still in their twenties, you would think too young for such serious business, but remember that boys went to college at fourteen then, and were ready for life at eighteen.

Benjamin Franklin was the oldest there—eighty-one now—and the wisest, too. There were some people, and not in America alone, who thought he was probably the wisest man in the world. He was certainly the best known of the delegates. Washington's greatness was something that filled the air, but outside America no one *knew* Washington. They had only heard about him. Everyone knew Franklin—in England, in Holland, in France—everywhere. Here is how William Pierce describes him:

Dr. Franklin is well known to be the greatest philosopher of the present age; all the operations of nature he seems to understand. The very heavens obey him, and the clouds yield up their lightning to be imprisoned in his rod. But what claim he has to the politican, posterity must determine.

It is certain that he does not shine much in public council—he is no speaker, nor does he seem to let politics engage his attention. He is, however, a most extraordinary man, and tells a story in a style more engaging than anything I ever heard. He is eighty-two years old [really just eighty-one] and possesses an activity of mind equal to a youth of twenty-five years of age.

The Reverend Manasseh Cutler gives us an even better picture of old Dr. Franklin. Cutler was not only a clergyman but also a famous botanist. As soon as he got to Philadelphia, he headed for Franklin as a bee heads for a hive. He found the doctor sitting out under a mulberry tree as he sipped tea with some friends from the Convention. Cutler saw:

A short, fat, trunched old man, in a plain Quaker dress, bald pate and short white locks, sitting without his hat under the tree, and as Mr. Gerry introduced me, he rose from his chair, took me by the hand, expressed his joy to see me, welcomed me to the city, and begged me to seat myself close to him. His voice was low, but his countenance open, frank and pleasing.

His daughter—"a gross and rather homely lady," says Cutler ungallantly—served tea. Grandchildren tumbled about the garden, and about their grandfather, too.

Franklin had a curiosity to show Dr. Cutler: a snake with two heads. Wouldn't it be funny, said Franklin, if the snake should be traveling along among the bushes, and one head wanted to go on one side a bush, and the other head on the other

Portrait of Benjamin Franklin, by Charles Willson Peale.

side. Suppose neither one would give away, and the snake would just stay there until it died!

That reminded him of something that had come up in the Convention . . . but then he remembered that he must not talk about the Convention.

After dark, they all went indoors, and Franklin showed Dr. Cutler some of his scientific and mechanical wonders. There was a machine that showed the circulation of the blood; a press for copying anything in just a minute; an artificial arm and hand to reach up to the top shelves of his vast library; a rocking chair with a fan for keeping off flies, worked by a foot pedal. All of them were Franklin's own inventions.

The Doctor seemed extremely fond of dwelling on philosophical subjects [Cutler added], and particularly that of natural history, while the other gentlemen were swallowed up with politics. This was a favorite circumstance to me, for almost the whole of his conversation was addressed to me; and I was highly delighted with the extensive knowledge he appeared to have of every subject, the brightness of his memory, and clearness and vivacity of all his mental faculties.

Notwithstanding his age, his manners are perfectly easy, and everything about him seems to diffuse an unrestrained freedom and happiness. He has an incessant vein of humor, accompanied with an uncommon vivacity, which seems as natural and involuntary as his breathing. . . .

But back to the Convention!

IV

It was on Monday, May 28 that the Convention really got going, passing on the credentials of members, and drawing up rules and deciding on secrecy, and what not. Best of all, Dr. Franklin felt well enough to come that day. This made it almost official!

The most important thing that happened that first day, though, was that James Madison decided to be a kind of unofficial secretary and keep a record of everything that was said. As soon as he came in, he took a chair right up front—but let him tell about it himself:

50

I chose a seat in front of the presiding member [that is, Washington] with the other members on my right hand and left hand. In this favorable position for hearing all that passed, I noted in terms legible and abbreviations and marks intelligible to myself, what was read from the Chair or spoken by the members.

And losing not a moment unnecessarily between the adjournment and reassembling of the Convention, I was enabled to write out my daily notes during the session or within a few finishing days after its close. . . . I was not absent a single day, nor more than a fraction of an hour in any day. . . .

Let us thank our lucky stars for Madison. If it weren't for him, we would never have known what went on in Philadelphia that summer. No one else kept a real record, and the members were careful not to write letters about the arguments and decisions—not even to their wives!

What a wonderful little fellow Madison was, just five feet four, and so quiet and modest you probably wouldn't notice him in a crowd. Yet he was sure to be just about the most important person in any gathering. Certainly he was, next to Washington himself, the most important man in the

Portrait of James Madison, by Gilbert Stuart.

Convention—the man who did more than anyone else to give us a Constitution.

He married late and didn't have any children of his own, but he is called the Father of the Constitution; perhaps that is enough fatherhood for any one person.

Mr. Pierce of Georgia—he came that very week and began making notes on his fellow delegates right away—wasn't fooled at all by Madison's soft voice and modest manners. Here is what he wrote:

> Mr. Madison is a character who has long been in public life; and what is very remarkable, every person seems to acknowledge his greatness. He blends together the profound politician with the scholar. In the management of every great question he evidently took the lead in the Convention. And though he cannot be called an orator, he is a most agreeable, eloquent, and convincing speaker.
>
> From a spirit of industry and application which he possesses in a most eminent degree, he always comes forward the best informed man on any point in debate. The affairs of the United States, he perhaps has the most correct knowledge of, of any man in the Union. He has been twice a Member of Congress, and was always thought one of the

ablest Members that ever sat in that Council.

Mr. Madison is about thirty-seven years of age, a gentleman of great modesty—with a remarkable sweet temper. He is easy and unreserved among his acquaintance, and has a most agreeable style of conversation.

Remember, the Virginians had put together a plan even before the Convention opened. That plan—Madison wrote it and Washington approved it—wiped out the old government and started over with a new one. The new government was to be truly national. That meant a government strong enough to manage all the things that national governments have always had to take care of: war and peace, and treaties, and commerce and trade, and money and taxes, and lands and Indians and things of that kind.

So Edmund Randolph opened the meeting with this neat Virginia plan. Though he hadn't written it, he was the Governor of Virginia, and very popular, and so it was natural enough to let him speak for the Virginians. Besides, no one knew quite where he stood on this matter of a strong or a weak government. Madison and Washington figured out that one way to get him on their side was to let him take credit for their plan.

Here was Randolph, then, reading out the Virginia proposals one after another. They quite took your breath away, these proposals, for if you put together all the ideas, you could easily see that they meant a new Constitution and a new nation, too. The plan said so, in so many words.

There was to be a national government, and it was to have real power—power to do everything that the States could not do. Under the old Confederation, there had been a Congress, but no President and no Court. The new plan called for a President and a Court as well as a Congress. And they weren't to be just figureheads, either, but to have real power.

This was strong medicine, stronger than most of the delegates had expected to take, certainly on the opening day. For a time, it threw them off balance. The delegates who wanted to see a real *nation* come out of this Convention were delighted; the delegates who still clung to the idea of all-important *States* were alarmed.

From the very beginning, the Convention shaped up—and divided—in this way. Whatever they were called, there were really only two sides arguing against each other. Let us call them the National Party and the States-Rights party.

One party wanted a strong central government that could hold its own among the other governments of the world. The other party thought that the States—New York and Connecticut and North Carolina and the rest—had been doing a pretty good job so far. They saw no reason to abandon them in favor of a new and untried system.

For a time, the Nationalists had things all their own way. For one thing, they had been smart enough to have a *plan*—that's always an advantage. For another, they had the best cause—the most sensible and the most logical one. And, finally, they had the ablest men in the Convention—the best brains and the best speakers.

They had Washington. He couldn't say anything because he sat up in the chair presiding over the Convention. But everyone knew where he stood. Much as he loved his own State, he hadn't fought in the Revolution for eight years just for Virginia alone. He had fought to make a nation. Everybody remembered the letter Washington had sent out at the end of the war, when he was ready to return to Mount Vernon. Americans, he wrote,

> . . . are not only surrounded with every thing which can contribute to the completion of private and domestic enjoyment, but Heaven has crowned all its other blessings by giving fairer opportunity for political happiness than any other Nation has ever been favored with. . . .

Yet . . . it is still their choice, and depends upon their conduct, whether they will be respectable and prosperous, or contemptible and miserable as a Nation.

This is the time of their political probation; this is the moment when the eyes of the world are turned upon them; this is the moment to establish or ruin their national character forever. This is the favorable moment to give such a tone to our Federal Government as will enable it to answer the ends of its institution.

Since that time, Washington had worked day and night for a stronger government. He sent letters to his friends all over the country—to Jay and Hamilton up in New York, to John Adams, to General Knox, to Madison in near-by Virginia. For heaven's sake, he told them, *do* something. Get on with the job. That is why he had gone to the Convention himself: to lend his influence and prestige to the effort to get a stronger government.

The Nationalists had Franklin, too—next to Washington the most famous member of the Convention. He was too old now to take an active part in discussions, but everyone knew where he stood. He was the man who had put together a colonial union back in 1763. He was the man who had drawn up the first "Articles of Confederation and Perpetual Union" at the very beginning of the Revolution—don't forget that, *Perpetual Union*.

Franklin had gone to France and soon all France was at his feet—all Europe, for that matter. Whenever a European thought of America, he thought of Dr. Franklin. And Europeans thought of *America*, not just of Pennsylvania.

When Franklin—carefully dressed in the brown velveteen suit he had worn ten years earlier, when he had been called hard names by that bully, Attorney-General Weddeburn—had signed the treaty of peace, it was a treaty for the independence of the *United States*.

The Nationalists had Madison, of course. We have already been introduced to him, and we know how strong he was, all by himself. As he sat up front and kept busy taking down everything that was said, you might suppose he'd have no time to say anything himself. But he did.

In fact, next to Gouverneur Morris, he said more than anyone else. Or maybe he just managed to remember every time he spoke, and to write it down. At any rate, there he was, thinking of everything and managing everything, always ready with the right idea at the right time, always working constantly to see that what the Convention put together would be a *Nation*.

58

After Madison, the man who did most to make sure that the new Constitution would provide a government that was strong and democratic was James Wilson of Pennsylvania. "James the Caledonian" he was called, because he came from Scotland (which was once known as Caledonia). Very Scottish he was, too—in his learning, in the way he spoke and even in his looks. Our friend Pierce was immensely impressed with him:

Mr. Wilson ranks among the foremost in legal and political knowledge. He has joined to a fine genius all that can set him off and show him to advantage. He is well acquainted with Man, and understands all the passions that influence him.

Government seems to have been his peculiar study. All the political institutions of the world he knows in detail, and can trace the causes and effects of every revolution from the earliest stages of the Grecian commonwealth down to the present time.

No man is more clear, copious and comprehensive than Mr. Wilson, yet he is no great orator. He draws the attention not by the charm of his eloquence, but by the force of his reasoning. He is about forty-five years old.

James Wilson

"Ranks foremost in legal knowledge"—how right Mr. Pierce was. Wilson knew all there was to know about the law. And when the Constitution was finally adopted and the new government set up, Washington placed him on the Supreme Court, where he belonged.

There was one other delegate who played a key part in making the nation: Alexander Hamilton of New York. Though barely thirty years old, he was already so famous it was hard to think of him as a young man. He had been born in the Leeward Islands in the Caribbean, of all places. When little more than a boy, he was sent by friends to New York for his education, to King's College. King's College is Columbia University now, and a statue of young Alexander Hamilton stands in front of the building named after him.

While he was in college, he couldn't keep out of politics. When the war came, he threw himself into it with tremendous enthusiasm. Washington had his eye on him, and in no time at all Hamilton was secretary to the Commander-in-Chief, writing his letters for him, and sometimes important official papers as well.

Wonderful to be next to Washington, you would think—and so it was. But Hamilton was not satisfied. Somehow, he was never satisfied with life, no matter what it brought him.

What he wanted now was to get into the fight. He "loved to hear the sound of bullets whistling about his ears." Washington let him have his way: he was in on the fighting at Yorktown, and at the end of it, he was called Colonel, which he enjoyed.

Now he lived in New York, practicing law and writing political articles for the newspapers. He had found time to marry the pretty daughter of General Schuyler, who was a great swell. All in all, Hamilton had done well for an immigrant boy without a penny to his name or any family to help him.

Everyone admired Hamilton; he was so brilliant, so handsome and so dashing. But not everyone liked him. Mr. Pierce, for example, makes clear his feelings from the way he described him:

> Colonel Hamilton is deservedly celebrated for his talents. He is a practitioner of the law, and reputed to be a finished scholar. To a clear and strong judgment he unites the ornaments of fancy; and while he is able, convincing and engaging in his eloquence, the heart and head sympathize in approving him.
>
> Yet there is something too feeble in his voice to be equal to the strains of oratory. It is my opinion that he is rather a convincing speaker, than a blazing orator.

New York Chamber of Commerce
Alexander Hamilton

Colonel Hamilton requires time to think; he enquires into every part of his subject with the searchings of philosophy, and when he comes forward he comes highly charged with interesting matter. There is no skimming over the surface of a subject with him; he must sink to the bottom to see what foundation it rests on.

His language is not always equal, sometimes didactic, at others light and tripping. His eloquence is not so defusive as to trifle with the senses, but he rambles just enough to strike and keep up the attention.

He is about thirty-three years old, of small stature, and lean. His manners are tinctured with stiffness, and sometimes with a degree of vanity that is highly disagreeable.

Poor Hamilton! He meant to cut quite a figure in the Convention, but he never had a chance. For New York sent two other delegates who disagreed with Hamilton on every single subject. Since each State had only one vote, Hamilton was boxed in. He made one long speech telling the members just what he would do if *he* could draw up the Constitution—no wonder Pierce thought he had "a degree of vanity"—and then he packed up and went home, the most sensible thing to do.

V

FOR TWO weeks, the Nationalists held the floor. Then the other side had its innings. Perhaps this sounds as if there were two teams lined up and taking turns. It was not that simple.

There *were* Nationalists—like Madison and Wilson—and there *were* champions of the rights of the States. But a good many others were now on one side, now on the other. Sometimes things got so mixed up that no one knew where he stood. Members would vote one way one day, and another way the next day.

All the same, one group in the Convention held

together and looked with suspicion on the rush toward nationalism. They knew a thing or two about nationalism, themselves, and they didn't like it.

Across the Atlantic, they saw all the Old World nations with their kings and their nobles and their armies and navies and their everlasting wars. And they concluded that America was better off without a strong national government. Say what you would about States like Connecticut or New Jersey, they did not set up kings or go around fighting wars.

The French minister to America, Monsieur Otto wrote that the people of Connecticut "have a character not to be equalled in any other part of the Continent, that they live in utmost simplicity and without any acquaintance with luxury, and that the people are happy."

Those who felt the States were more important than the nation held to this great point: that the people were happy as they were.

Certainly—they said—certainly we need a general government to deal with other nations, and to take charge of such things as the public lands out West or the Indians, to see to it that the mail is delivered, and that we all use the same kind of money. But what more do we need?

Why not let the States manage their own affairs

in peace and quiet? They'd done a pretty good job of it so far. Peace and Plenty; that's what you would say when you looked at Connecticut or Pennsylvania or Maryland. Peace and Plenty and Contentment!

Who were the spokesmen for this party that wanted to keep the States at the center of things? They had no Washington or Franklin, no names as great as these, but they had men who were not to be sneezed at.

First, we have to introduce the man who drew up and presented their plan, "Judge" Paterson of New Jersey. Born in Ireland, he had been brought to America as a boy, studied—like so many members of the Convention—at Princeton College, then turned to law and politics. Pierce was very much impressed by him:

> Mr. Paterson is one of those kings of men whose powers break in upon you, and create wonder and astonishment. He is a man of great modesty, with looks that bespeak talents of no great extent, but he is a classic, a lawyer, and an orator—and of a disposition so favorable to his advancement that every one seemed ready to exalt him with their praises.
>
> He is very happy in the choice of time and manner of engaging in a debate, and never

speaks but when he understands his subject well.

Pierce was right to be impressed. Before long, Paterson was Governor of his State, and then Justice of the Supreme Court of the United States.

An even more interesting character was old Roger Sherman of Connecticut. He was along in his sixties, and that was very old, then. This self-made man had once been a farmer and a shoemaker.

He wasn't much to look at, Mr. Sherman. Pierce thought him "the oddest-shaped character I ever remember to have met with." But everyone trusted him, which is what counted.

Pierce came from Georgia and didn't always find it easy to understand Yankees. So he described Roger Sherman in this way:

He is awkward, un-meaning, and unaccountably strange in his manner. But in his train of thinking there is something regular, deep and comprehensive. Yet the oddity of his address, the vulgarisms that accompany his public speaking, and that strange New England cant which runs through his public as well as his private speaking, make everything that is connected with him grotesque and laughable.

Roger Sherman

And yet, he deserves infinite praise—no man has a better heart or a clearer head. If he cannot embellish, he can furnish thoughts that are wise and useful. He is an able politician, and extremely artful in accomplishing any particular object. It is remarked that he seldom fails. . . .

The third leader of the States-Rights group was one of those bores who are so full of themselves that they can never stop talking. That was Luther Martin of Maryland—another Princeton man, by the way. There was nothing wrong with his brains; he was as smart as they came. But how he did go on, and on, and on, until all you wanted was to get away from that voice grinding out at you. He bored Mr. Pierce, just as he bored everyone else:

> Mr. Martin was educated for the Bar, and is Attorney-General for the State of Maryland. This gentleman possesses a good deal of information, but he has a very bad delivery, and so extremely prolix, that he never speaks without tiring the patience of all who hear him.

Still and all, Martin had his points. He was a first-rate lawyer; he was a tough fighter. He was even a good companion when he forgot politics and went on to tell about his law cases.

Some members of the Convention seemed to be on both sides at once. It wasn't that they didn't know their own minds. It was rather that they were torn two ways. They understood the need for a strong national government, yet they feared that if the government was really strong it might be used to trample the rights of the people.

George Mason of Virginia belonged in this camp. Like a good many men of that day, he was both rich and radical. Men like that aren't seen so often now. He was a great planter, and owned many slaves, but he was ardently devoted to democracy and to liberty.

Mason was one of the most famous men in the Convention because he had written the Virginia Bill of Rights—the Bill of Rights that was copied in almost every State and served as a model for the one that went into the Constitution of the United States.

Another of these fence-sitters was Hugh Williamson of North Carolina. He wasn't really very important, but he was such an odd character that you wouldn't want to miss him and you shan't. He was the kind of man you simply don't see anymore. Pierce had little to say about Williamson. "There is a great degree of good humor and pleasantry in his character, and in his manners there is a strong trait of the gentleman." That is all.

But the French minister, Monsieur Otto, hit him off better. "Doctor, and one-time Professor of Astronomy," he wrote, "he is bizarre to excess." It is hard to get to know Williamson's character, Otto said, and then added, "Maybe he hasn't got one."

Williamson had plenty of character, all right. As a young man, he had studied for the ministry, and even preached for a while. Then he gave it up for mathematics and astronomy. That didn't seem to get him anywhere, so he sailed off to Holland to study medicine, and came back a full-fledged doctor from the University of Utrecht. Soon he tired of medicine, too, and decided to go into business. So he settled down as a merchant in North Carolina.

When the war came along, there was little use for merchants, but a dire need for doctors. So Williamson got out his pills and his medical instruments, went into the army, finally becoming surgeon-general of the North Carolina troops. As one might suspect, this rolling stone ended up in an entirely different State with an entirely different job: in New York, of all places, as a man of letters.

For a while, they were at it hammer and tongs in the Convention, the Nationalists and the States-Rights men. Wilson and Madison and Morris kept pushing for a real national government, and Hamilton scared everyone with his high-falutin' notions, and Gunning Bedford of Delaware said you fellows be careful or the small States will call in outside help, and then he apologized for the awful words and said he didn't mean them.

Luther Martin got up and talked and talked for two whole days. "It might have gone on for two months," wrote one of the delegates, "had not the Convention showed its boredom."

By the end of June, matters were so sticky that Dr. Franklin thought it was time to call on Heaven for help:

In this situation of this Assembly, groping as it were in the dark to find political truth, and scarce able to distinguish it when presented to us, how has it happened, Sir, that we have not hitherto once thought of humbly applying to the Father of light to illuminate our understandings? In the beginning of the contest with Great Britain, when we were sensible of danger, we had daily prayer in this room for the divine protection. Our prayers, Sir, were heard and they were graciously answered. . . .

And have we now forgotten that powerful friend? Or do we imagine that we no longer need His assistance? I have lived, Sir, a long time, and the longer I live, the more convincing proofs I see of this truth—*that God governs in the affairs of men.*

And if a sparrow cannot fall to the ground without His notice, is it probable that an empire can rise without His aid? We have been assured, Sir, in the sacred writings, that "except the Lord build the House they labor in vain that build it."

I firmly believe this; and I also believe that without His concurring aid we shall succeed in this political building no better than the builders of Babel. We shall be divided by our little partial local interests; our projects will be confounded, and we ourselves shall become a reproach and a byword down to future ages.

It really seemed for a time as if the Convention would break up, and on this issue of large and small States, too. The leaders of the small States had somehow got it into their heads that their States were in danger. They thought that if the Nationalists had their way, the big States would eat up the little ones.

However unreasonable it might have been, that is the way they felt. They held the whip hand, too. They could always pack up and go home. Then there would be no Constitution at all, and there might not even be a government. Clearly the Nationalists had to give in—on some matters anyway—because they were the ones who wanted to keep things going.

What happened was that a committee got together and came up with a very simple solution. At least, it seems like a simple solution to us.

Since the little States were so afraid of what might happen to them if the large States had more votes in Congress, let them have the protection they wanted. Give every State, little and big alike, the same vote in the upper house of Congress—which we call the Senate. That way, the big States could never ride rough-shod over the little ones. And to make things doubly sure, let the Constitution "guarantee" to every state "a republican form of government."

That's the way it was finally arranged, and that's the way it is today. One house of Congress—the House of Representatives—represents the people generally. The other one, the Senate, represents the States.

As we look back on it now, we wonder that men quarreled so over this matter. After all, there was not really any danger to the States from the national government, or to the small States from the big ones. Nobody was going to hurt Delaware or Rhode Island or New Jersey just because they were small. And giving each State two Senators really meant very little, in the end. Nowadays, Senators don't vote for Vermont or Ohio or Kansas; they vote most of the time along with their party, no matter which State they come from.

But no one thought of political parties in 1787.

So here it was: a compromise that turned out

not to mean very much. But it let the Convention get on with the job.

Once the question was settled, everyone could take a deep breath and knuckle down to work again. How they worked, those hot July days! One by one, the problems that had loomed up like mountains faded away or became little hillocks easy enough to get over.

Now there came a good omen, too. The delegates from little New Hampshire arrived at long last. New Hampshire was so poor that the two men had had to pay their own way. But no matter; fortunately Mr. Langdon was rich enough to pay for both of them! Now only little Rhode Island was out. And there was a general feeling that Rhode Island could stew in its own juice.

By the end of the month, the delegates had got so far that they decided it was time to call a halt. They would put together everything they had done, and see how it looked. This job they handed over to a committee; then they took a recess for ten days.

It was a welcome interlude. Some of the delegates who lived nearby went to see their families, who were feeling pretty neglected by now. Others took the chance to see something of Philadelphia and the lovely countryside around it, to take picnics along the Schuylkill River, to revisit the battlefields where they had fought so hard just a few years back.

Washington went out to near-by Valley Forge, where so many of his soldiers had frozen and starved that terrible winter of 1778. It was so beautiful now, the grain almost ripe and the orchards heavy with fruit. That night Washington wrote in his Diary that

Whilst Mr. Morris was fishing, I rid over the whole old cantonment of the American Army in the winter of 1777 and 8, visited all the works which were in ruins; and the incampments in woods where the grounds had not been cultivated.

On my return, observing some farmers at work, and entering into conversation with them, I received the following information with respect to the mode of cultivating buckwheat and the application of the grain.

He always was more interested in farming than in anything else. One day, he rode out to see a nearby vineyard on the banks of the Schuylkill, with his old friend, Daniel of St. Thomas Jenifer. What a name! His father had been named Daniel, and he had a brother named Daniel, so there must have been quite a bit of confusion in that household.

77

That ten-day vacation cleared the air. When the delegates buckled down to work again, they were in good spirits. For now the committee had reported, and lo and behold! they had a Constitution. There were still all kinds of questions to be answered—important questions, too, some of them—but there was no longer any danger that the Convention would break up and go home.

One question still in the minds of many concerned the western lands and new States. Remember that the United States, in 1787, stretched westward all the way to the Mississippi River, and that most of the land west of the Appalachian Mountains belonged to the United States, not to individual States. What was to become of it? That was easy enough: Settle it, and make it into new States.

So far, there were still only the thirteen States, but everyone knew that couldn't last long. Perhaps no one foresaw fifty States, but already Vermont was clamoring to get in, and Kentucky too. It was clear that the thirteen States would be doubled before long.

But it wasn't that simple—or was it? Suppose you divided the West up into a lot of States and let them all join the Union. Wouldn't there be so many that in the end they would swamp the original thirteen? Wouldn't it be more sensible to arrange things so the original thirteen States would

Daniel of St. Thomas Jenifer

always hold the whip hand?

The idea was not really unreasonable. What should you think if, after you had fought a Revolution and written a Constitution, a lot of newcomers jostle you out of your seat, and took over?

Of course the answer is that it doesn't make any

difference what you would think. Either the new States would come in as equals, or they would set up on their own. And it was certainly better to have them in the Union than outside it.

That question was settled, and settled in the right way. Ohio and Iowa and Alabama and Colorado—and your own State too—could all come into the Union as equals. Actually that hasn't done any harm—not to Massachusetts or Pennsylvania or the other original States.

Next, there was the problem of the President. You take a President for granted, now. What else can we have? What would we do with the White House if there were no President? But in 1787, there wasn't any President, or any White House, either.

There were governors of States, but when it came to the head of a country, all anyone could think of was a King or an Emperor. He might be insane, like the King of Denmark, but he was still King, and you pretended that he read all the State papers and made all of the decisions.

He might be starting a war just because it pleased him, like the King of Prussia or the Czar of Russia, but that couldn't be helped. He sat on a throne and had a crown on his head, so you went out and fought the wars, and got killed if necesasry, without having any say in the matter. Whoever heard of getting along without any kind of King at all?

Well, Americans had managed to get rid of one King, George III of England, and they didn't fancy another. Instead, they invented something new: a President! A President who would be elected, instead of being born to his position. A President who could be sent home after four years —sooner if he didn't behave himself. (All of them have behaved themselves, and none has been sent home before his term was up.) A President who had only the powers that the people gave to him.

The most important single thing about this invention was something everyone knew, but no one mentioned—not in the Convention, anyway. It was this: The members of the Convention couldn't even think about a President without thinking about General Washington. There he sat, day after day, looking every inch the great man. Every king, said John Adams, looked like a valet next to him!

Everybody in the Convention—and out of it— knew that if ever there was a new government, Washington would be at the head of it. If there was to be a President, it would be Washington. And, of course, it was!

So when the Convention argued about the President—how long he should hold office, and what powers he should have, and all that—they always had Washington in mind. And because everybody trusted Washington, and knew that he would never do anything he shouldn't, they gave the President more power than they really meant to. They modeled the office on the man.

That was fine for the office, but it was sometimes pretty hard on the men who had to fill it. They weren't all Washingtons.

On a Wednesday in the middle of August, as the Conven-

Fitch's steamboat

tion discussed trade and navigation, an event took place that proved the necessity of union better than all the arguments of all the delegates and showed one way it would come about, too. On that day, the inventor John Fitch ran his steamboat up and down the Delaware River.

There it was for everybody to see, the wheels churning and the smoke coming out of the smokestacks on the little boat. It was the first steamboat in the world. It would be twenty years before

on the Delaware River opposite Philadelphia.

Robert Fulton launched the *Clermont* on the Hudson River. And it would be another twenty years before steamboats tied together the East and the West, the North and the South, into a single system. No one saw this at the time. No one appreciated the wonder of John Fitch's invention, or how it would change history.

Poor John Fitch. He tried in vain to get people to listen to him. Finally, in despair, he went out west, and died.

83

VI

Now it was September, and the members of the Convention were tired. Ever since the end of May, they had been at work, cooped up in one room in hot Philadelphia. They wanted to finish up and go home. Some of them had not seen their families for almost four months. Most of the big questions had been settled. Members now wrangled only about details, and after a while that got to be a bore.

For they really had a Constitution.

What finally had emerged was, of course, a compromise—a compromise which is the federal system. The new government was neither entirely national nor entirely State.

In some matters, the national government was in control—in such things as war, treaties, commerce, public lands and the post office. In other matters, the States were very much in control—in all local matters like schools or roads or town government, for example.

And—this was what was really clever—neither government was really "over" the other one. Each one was "over" the individual citizen. When the national government passed a law, let's say a tax, it could go right to every person and make him pay up. When the State government passed a law, let's say a law requiring all children to go to school, it could enforce that law directly on all the parents and children in the State.

Each government had its own place and its own powers, and neither one interfered with the other. All in all, it was the most complicated political machine ever invented, and it took a pretty smart people to make it work.

Early in September, the Convention handed the whole thing over to a committee to whip it into final shape. This "Committee on Style" included men like Gouverneur Morris and Madison and even Hamilton, who had come back from New York to be in at the finish.

The committee let Morris do the job. A fine job he made of it, too, for he knew how to turn a phrase and how to write clearly and sharply. Of course, the Convention had already agreed on the Constitution. Now the job was to get the words in the right order, to put in the punctuation, to dot the *i*'s and cross the *t*'s. But not entirely. Every so often, Morris slipped in a word of his own that he thought was an improvement—and usually it was.

Above all, Morris liked a bit of a flourish. He remembered Jefferson's wonderful introduction to the Declaration of Independence; you know: "When in the course of human events. . . ." and he thought the Constitution ought to have something like that, too, something to start it off right, with both dignity and elegance. So he wrote a Preamble, and that is the part of the Constitution you and all the rest of us know best. Morris made his mark on history after all:

> We, the People of the United States, in Order to form a more perfect Union, establish Justice, insure domestic Tranquility, provide for the common defense, promote the general Welfare, and secure the Blessings of Liberty to ourselves and our Posterity, do ordain and establish this Constitution for the United States of America.

Portrait of Thomas Jefferson, by Charles Willson Peale.

Now it was mid-September, and it was all finished, all but a little canter at the end. Suddenly everybody was pleased. They'd done it, after all! Who would have thought it?

A few of the members who weren't pleased—like that old curmudgeon Luther Martin, and those two New Yorkers who had hobbled Hamilton all along—had gone home.

Three other members rose to explain why they couldn't sign the Constitution—just three: Mason of Virginia, Randolph of Virginia and Elbridge Gerry of Massachusetts.

Everyone respected Mason, and listened carefully when he gave his explanation. He objected chiefly because the Constitution did not have a Bill of Rights, and after all, he was an expert on Bills of Rights. As it turned out, he was right, too, and the first thing the new government did was to add a Bill of Rights.

Randolph's position was a bit more awkward. After all, he had introduced the Virginia Plan in the first place, and it seemed a bit odd that he would not put his name to it now. But that was the way with Randolph: never knowing his own mind, and always on both sides of every question, and worried to death about what people would think.

As for Gerry—no one much minded what he did. He was called a "Grumbletonian," a man who was against everything except what he himself proposed. He ended up as Vice-President of the United States, so his opposition to the Constitution couldn't have been very serious after all.

Nobody in the Convention was happier than Dr. Franklin. He knew he hadn't much longer to live, but it was something to have lived long enough to see this. Just imagine, he had been born back in 1706, when the Colonies were so new and small that it wasn't at all certain that they would survive. And he had lived to see them grow and become strong and prosperous, and win their independence. Now he was to see them unite as a nation.

He hoped everybody realized just how wonderful this all was, and that everybody would join in to make it a success. He had written down a few thoughts and now he got up to read them. But he was too tired, so Mr. Wilson read what he had written. Here it is:

Mr. President, I confess that there are several parts of this Constitution which I do not at present approve, but I am not sure I shall never approve them. For having lived long, I have experienced many instances of being obliged by better information, or fuller consideration, to change opinions even on important subjects, which I once thought right, but found to be otherwise.

It is therefore that the older I grow, the more apt I am to doubt my own judgment, and to pay more respect to the judgment of others.

Most men indeed, as well as most sects in religion, think themselves in possession of all truth, and that wherever others differ from them it is so far error. . . .

But though many private persons think almost as highly of their own infallibility as of that of their sect, few express it so naturally as a certain French lady who in a dispute with her sister said, "I don't know how it happens, Sister, but I meet with nobody but myself that's always in the right."

In these sentiments, Sir, I agree to this Constitution with all its faults, if they are such. . . . I doubt too whether any other Convention we can obtain, may be able to make a better Constitution.

For when you assemble a number of men to have the advantage of their joint wisdom, you inevitably assemble with those men all their prejudices, their passions, their errors of opinion, their local interest, and their selfish views. From such an assembly can a perfect production be expected?

It therefore astonishes me, Sir, to find this system approaching so near to perfection as it does; and I think it will astonish our enemies. . . .

Thus I consent, Sir, to this Constitution because I expect no better and because I am not sure that it is not the best. . . .

On the whole, Sir, I can not help expressing a wish that every member of the Convention who may still have objections to it, would with me, on this occasion, doubt a little of his own infallibility, and to make manifest our unanimity, put his name to this instrument.

Now Washington put the solemn question, and every single State voted "Aye." So it was "Done by the unanimous consent of the States present, the seventeenth day of September, 1787."

One by one, the members came forward to sign the document. Each dipped the quill pen into the ink bottle and wrote carefully to make certain his name could be read. Washington himself had left the chair to put his own name to it. As the last members signed, Franklin had a final word to say, a final word that was the perfect tribute:

Dr. Franklin, looking towards the President's chair, at the back of which a rising sun happened to be painted, observed to a few members near him, that painters had found it difficult to distinguish in their art a rising from a setting sun.

"I have," said he, "often and often in the course of this session, and the vicissitudes of my hopes and fears as to its issue, looked at that behind the President without being able to tell whether it was rising or setting. But now, at length, I have the happiness to know that it is a rising and not a setting sun."

That night, the members dined together for the last time, and took leave of each other. And Washington "retired to meditate on the momentous work which had been executed."

The Signing of the Constitution.

VII

IT WAS one thing to write a Constitution; it was another to get the American people to accept it. Or most of them anyway. The Convention had decided that as soon as nine of the thirteen States accepted the Constitution, it should go into effect. Then the old Confederation would go out of business, and the new United States get under way.

So now it was up to the delegates to see to it that the States *did* accept the new Constitution—all of them, if possible, but at least nine of them.

Remember that all during the debates, no one outside the Convention had heard a word about what was going on. All kinds of rumors flew: The Convention planned to set up a King; they would set up three separate Confederations instead of one; they were quarreling and on the point of breaking up. Everything would happen; nothing would happen. The Constitution was a triumph; the Constitution was a failure. . .

Now the Constitution was there for everyone to read, or at least for everyone to talk about. It was up to the members of the Convention to defend their work and to win support for it.

Back home they went—no rest for them—to explain what they had been about, all those weeks in Philadelphia. Back home to meet criticism, to win over enemies and to rally friends.

Questions came thick and fast. Well, sir, what did the Convention mean by *this?* And, what did it mean by *that?* Why did it give the President so much power? Why didn't it give the President more power? Where was the capitol to be? What was all this about a District of Columbia? Who knows what might happen there, with no States to watch over it! Why did the Constitution take away so much power from the States? Why did it leave so much power in the States? Why didn't it say something about slavery? Why? Why? Why?

How easy it was to ask questions and demand answers right off, just as if the Convention hadn't argued these very matters day after day, all summer long!

And yet it was all very exciting, and pretty wonderful, too, when we stop to think about it. For here was something really new under the sun. Washington explained it as well as anyone. He said, in a letter to one of his English friends:

> We exhibit at present the *novel and astonishing spectacle* of a whole people deliberating calmly on what form of government will be the most conducive to their happiness.

"The novel and astonishing spectacle"—that's just what it was. Americans in every town and village and country crossroads, in every inn and store and church, talked about the kind of government they meant to have. The newspapers were full of it. Printers were busy running off pamphlets by the dozen, all signed with fancy names—"Publius" or "Pro Bono Publico" or "The Maryland Farmer."

It was like a presidential election of today, though without the parades and fanfare and salesmanship. It was also an example of how Americans went about the business of governing themselves. And in 1787, *only* Americans could do this.

At first, everything went swimmingly. One

State convention after another met and accepted the Constitution—little Delaware, New Jersey, Georgia—without a single contrary vote. Note that these were "small" States. By now, there had been a complete about-face. It was the small States that were most eager to have the new Constitution, and the big States that raised all the objections.

The first real fight came in Pennsylvania.

To the farmers of that State, almost anything that went on in Philadelphia was suspect anyway— just as even today, a good many Illinois farmers don't quite trust Chicago, and a good many of the inhabitants of the villages of upstate New York have deep suspicions of whatever goes on in New York City.

But in the end, the arguments of James Wilson and the influence of Benjamin Franklin carried the day, and Pennsylvania fell into line. So, too, did Connecticut—now Roger Sherman was all for the Constitution! That made five States already.

In Massachusetts, opponents of the Constitution put up a tough fight. Once again, it looked as if the farmers were against the city people—Boston, this time, and the proud port of Salem. What made it hard was that the most popular of all the Bostonians, old Sam Adams, seemed to line up with the folks who were against the Constitution.

If you followed the arguments closely you could

tell that the farmers were really not so afraid of the Constitution as of the men who had written it. They were suspicious of anything that was new; they thought that something was being put over on them. Listen to one of them, named Amos Singletary:

> These lawyers and men of learning and monied men, that talk so finely and gloss over matters so smoothly, to make us poor illiterate people swallow down the pill, expect to get into Congress themselves.
>
> They expect to be managers of this Constitution, and get all the powers and all the money into their own hands. And then they will swallow up all us little folks, like the great Leviathan. . . . Yes, just as the whale swallowed Jonah.

Week after week, the people of Massachusetts were at it, hammer and tongs. Then someone thought up a way out. Most likely it was Governor Hancock. Remember how he wrote his name in such big letters under the Declaration of Independence that to this day we speak of a signature as a "John Hancock."

The solution for Massachusetts was very simple: Vote for the Constitution, but *recommend* lots of changes and improvements. This saved face for everybody. Those who did approve the Constitution could cheerfully accept the good advice. They could say, "Yes, we will do our best." And those who did not approve the Constitution at all could go home and say, "We did our best. We made them agree to a lot of changes!"

Massachusetts made six States. Soon Maryland and South Carolina came tumbling in, and there were eight. Now only one to go. Three States were holding conventions: New Hampshire, New York and Virginia. Any one of them would bring the number up to nine, and thus make the Constitution come alive.

Actually, it wasn't quite that simple.

Nine States had to agree, according to the Convention. But in fact everybody knew that it couldn't be just any nine. For imagine a United States without New York or Virginia!

In 1787, Virginia was far and away the largest American State—twice as large as any other. As for New York, it sat right in the middle of the thirteen States, dividing New England from all the rest. No, the United States *might* have got under way without Connecticut or Georgia, let us say, but it couldn't possibly get under way without Virginia and New York.

It was Virginia that put on the full-dress debate. That was as it should be. What with Washington and Madison, Virginia had done more than any other State to make certain that there would be a Constitution. But remember that two of the Virginians refused to sign it at the very end. They were George Mason and Governor Randolph. Randolph was *really* on the fence. He didn't know which way to turn, but finally he flopped over and came up on the side of the Constitution. Old George Mason was made of sterner stuff. He didn't give an inch.

It was not Mason, however, who led the fight on the Constitution, but Patrick Henry. Everybody knows about him; everybody remembers his famous words: "Give me liberty or give me death." He was Virginia's greatest orator—maybe the greatest in all America—and what is more to the point, he was probably the most popular man in Virginia.

Here then was Patrick Henry thundering against the Constitution with all his eloquence. What a dangerous government it was: Why, it was worse than anything George III had ever thought of! Just think: no limitation on the number of terms a President could serve, or, for that matter, a Congressman either. Why, the President would turn into a King and all the Senators into Lords! Just think: no limit to the salaries Congressmen could vote themselves. Why, they would all end

Patrick Henry

up richer than nabobs from India! Just think:
Congress could govern the District of Columbia
just as it pleased. Why, in no time at all, government there would be as tyrannical as under Louis
XIV of France!

Day after day, Patrick Henry went on. Terrible

things were in store for the American people if they accepted this Constitution!

But Henry didn't have things all his own way, not by a long shot. Madison was there, talking common sense all the time instead of the nonsense that Patrick Henry talked. And a young man named John Marshall was there. One day he would be Chief Justice of the United States. He was ready now to defend the new Constitution. All in all, the defenders of the Constitution more than held their own.

In New York, too, the going was hard. Almost everybody in New York City was in favor of the Constitution—merchants and workingmen alike. But in the villages and farms along the Hudson River, and westward along the Mohawk River, there was a different opinion. These people didn't usually see eye to eye with the New Yorkers, and they were pretty suspicious of the Constitution. But what could they do?

There was Hamilton holding forth, day after day, making the Constitution seem so right, so much the common sense of the matter, that it was hard to hold out against him. Then, too, there was the awful thought: suppose Virginia ratified, and there would be a new United States—and New York would be left out.

Then, at the end of June, everything happened

at once. First New Hampshire fell into line—that made nine States. Then, on the very same day, New York and Virginia both voted to accept the Constitution. That settled it. Eleven States had voted to be the United States.

Swift horsemen brought the news to General Washington at Mount Vernon—first the good news from his own State of Virginia; then the good news from New York and New Hampshire.

"The great Governor of the Universe has led us too long and too far on the road to happiness and glory to forsake us in the midst of it," Washington had once said. Now he could be sure that the great Governor had not forsaken the American people.

How his eyes lit up and his heart leaped within him as he looked back over the long, hard years from Lexington and Concord and Bunker Hill, the retreat through New Jersey, the crossing of the icy Delaware, the struggle for Philadelphia, the cruel winter at Valley Forge, the triumph at Yorktown—then the struggle for union, and the Philadelphia Convention.

Who would have thought these little States would somehow weather the storm? Who would have thought that they would come through to victory not only in war but in peace? Now there would be a nation. Now there would be a United States of America!

VIII

By good luck, the news about Virginia and New York came just in time for the Fourth of July celebrations. What good timing! There had been Fourth of July celebrations every year, but never one like this.

In New York, ten white horses dragged the good ship *Alexander Hamilton* up and down the narrow streets of the little city. Its guns fired thirteen salutes, while everybody marched in a huge parade with floats and wagons and soldiers on horseback. Only the women and children were left to cheer them on.

Boston! Baltimore! Charleston! Everywhere there were parades and military displays and fireworks, and dinners where everybody had to keep bobbing up and down drinking thirteen toasts. But it was Philadelphia that put on the biggest and the best of the celebrations. And that was natural enough, for after all, it was in Philadelphia that the nation had been born.

It was a hasty affair; the word that Virginia and New York had accepted the Constitution did not reach Philadelphia until the end of June. There were just a few days left for Judge Wilson and Judge Hopkinson and their friends to arrange a proper celebration. But the whole city pitched in to help.

The workers built floats; the teachers organized their pupils—the boys, anyway—to march with banners and flags. Veterans got out their uniforms to be pressed and somehow fitted. The clergy thought up suitable prayers and James Wilson worked up a speech. Little Francis Hopkinson— he was a judge who wrote poetry and music on the side—put together an "Ode" proper for the great occasion.

July fourth dawned bright and clear, not too hot and with a brisk south wind. The paraders began to assemble early in the morning—five thousand of them, no less. Soon all those not in the parade were lining the streets, jostling for a good position. All the farmers had come in from the country. Their horses stood tied to convenient trees or hitchingposts, and switched their tails to whisk off the flies.

The celebration was announced by the great bell in the steeple of Christ Church. And by a roaring salute from the cannon of the good ship *Rising Sun*, anchored at the foot of Market Street. And then by ten other ships, all berthed along Water Street, each flying a white flag with the name of one of the States in gold letters. All day long, a stiff south wind kept the flags fluttering in the breeze.

What a parade! First, the soldiers and veterans,

Federal Procession, New York City, July 1788.

led by nine officers with white plumes in their cocked hats. Then the floats. Each guild of skilled workers, each group in the government, or army, or navy, or the social life of the city, had its own float. Eighty-eight of them altogether—just imagine, in a little town of only fifty thousand or so—and each float more dazzling than the last.

Even a stranger would know all about Philadelphia by the time he had seen and heard this parade. He would know who the people were, and what they did for a living, and the things they were most proud of.

The boat-builders had a float, and the ship-carpenters, the rope-makers, the cabinet-makers, the house-painters, the bricklayers, the blacksmiths and the wheelwrights and the glove-makers. Even the sign-painters and the spinning-wheel makers had floats of their own. And all the members of the guilds—we would call them unions now—marched along behind, waving banners and singing songs and shouting to their families and friends.

The printers had one of the best of all the floats: a stage with a printing press all complete. There printers set up and printed copies of Francis Hopkinson's "Ode," and threw them out to the crowds. And what is more, they had pigeons who flew off with copies of the "Ode" tied to their legs. These birds flew all over Philadelphia and far beyond, so it could be said that Mr. Hopkinson's poetry really came down from Heaven!

Some of the floats were like fairy palaces.

Here was number 34: "The New Roof" or "The Grand Federal Edifice," drawn by no less than ten white horses. This splendid float held a building with a dome supported by thirteen columns and decorated with thirteen stars. Ten of the columns were complete; three not quite finished. That was for the ten States that had ratified the Constitution, and the three that hadn't. (The people here did not know about New Hampshire yet; otherwise it would have been eleven.) On top of the dome was a great cornucopia, the symbol of plenty. And around the base of the pedestal were engraved the words: *"IN UNION THE FABRIC STANDS FIRM."*

Number 33 was just as magnificent: "The Federal Ship Union," it was called. And it was a real ship, over thirty feet long—imagine hauling that through the narrow streets of Philadelphia! The ship was commanded by four midshipmen in full uniform and a crew of twenty-five, who went through all the motions of trimming the sails, hauling in rope and casting anchor, just as if they were at sea.

Perhaps the handsomest float of all was number 13: "The Constitution." It was an immense carriage built in the form of an eagle. Its body was painted light blue, its breast decorated with thirteen silver stars and a shield of thirteen red and white stripes. What a wonderful idea! And in the carriage sat the Chief Justice of the State of Pennsylvania, and all the other justices in their black robes, looking very solemn indeed.

When the parade was over—and it took hours—there were dinners and speech-making and fireworks. And of course, Mr. Hopkinson's "Ode." It was Mr. Hopkinson's day, all right—one might almost suppose he had written the Constitution!

There were, in fact, a lot of Mr. Hopkinsons—he was a bit like Benjamin Franklin that way. There was Judge Hopkinson, who was a judge of sea law, and who had had a float all to himself and wore a gold anchor hanging down from his green hat. And there was Mr. Hopkinson the chemist, and Mr. Hopkinson the inventor, and Mr. Hopkinson the musician. And then there was Mr. Hopkinson the poet.

He had already written one poem for this happy occasion. It was called "The New Roof," and it went along so well you couldn't keep from singing it:

> Up! up! with the rafters; each frame is a State;
> Now nobly they rise! their span, too, how
> great!

From the north to the south, o'er the whole
    they extend,
And rest on the walls, whilst the walls they
    defend;
For our roof we will raise, and our song
    still shall be,
Combined in strength, yet as citizens free.

Huzza! my brave boys, our work is complete;
This world shall admire Columbia's fair
    feat;
Its strength against tempest and time shall
    be proof,
And thousands shall come to dwell under
    one roof;
While we drain the deep bowl, our toast still
    shall be,
Our government firm, and our citizens free.

Now, at the end of the great celebration, he read
his "Ode." It was a solemn affair, not nearly so
easy to read as "The New Roof," and not so much
fun, either. One stanza will be enough for us:

See where Columbia sits alone,
And from her star-bespangled throne,
Beholds the gay procession move along,
And hears the trumpet and the choral song.
She hears her sons rejoice;
Looks into future times, and sees,
The numerous blessings heaven decrees;
And with her plaudit joins the general voice.

IX

Now IT was a year later, the spring of 1789. For the third time, George Washington was making ready to leave his beloved Mount Vernon and point his horse's head to the north.

The first time had been in 1775, when he had put on his uniform and buckled on his sword and made his way to Philadelphia to command the American armies fighting for independence. The second time it had been to Philadelphia again, to see if he could help save the nation he had helped create, by making a new Constitution.

Both times he had done his duty, and then gone quietly home to Mount Vernon to farm his neglected acres.

Poor Washington, was he never to know rest or retirement or a private life?

Now they had made him President, just as everyone knew they would. Every single vote had been for Washington. What could he do about that? He didn't want to be President. He had, he said, "no wish but that of living and dying an honest man on my own farm."

Washington had just settled down on his plantation along the bank of the Potomac, to get it into shape after long years of neglect. Now here he was expected to leave home again, to take up once more the heavy burden of public duty, or, as he put it, "in the evening of a life nearly consumed with public cares, to quit a peaceful abode for an ocean of difficulties."

But when did Washington ever fail to respond to the call of duty? He saw to the spring planting; he went off to near-by Fredericksburg to say good-by to his aged mother; he borrowed a few thousand dollars to pay up his bills and meet his expenses. Then he rode off for this last great adventure.

Washington left Mount Vernon on the seventeenth of April, the pleasantest month of the year in Virginia, with the roses in bloom, the fruit trees

Washington's reception on the bridge at Trenton in 1789, on his way to be inaugurated first President of the United States.

filling the air with their fragrance, and the birds flitting in and out of the vines. Everything was fresh and green and lovely.

Washington started out with two old friends of Revolutionary days. Their path took them over familiar ground—ground where they had fought many a battle, and suffered many a defeat. But what a difference now! It was one long triumphal procession all the way to New York. The whole nation had given itself up to celebration and rejoicing, and the people seemed beside themselves with excitement.

Every town presented the same scene: flags everywhere, the streets decorated with red, white and blue bunting. Townspeople lined the roads, swinging their hats and cheering at the top of their voices. Bands played, church bells rang, cannons fired salutes. Little girls threw flowers before the President. Hard-bitten veterans of the war pranced up on their horses to escort their old commander-in-chief to the next town.

Never before had there been such an outpouring of affection and of worship for any man. Alexandria, Georgetown, Baltimore, Wilmington, Chester, Philadelphia—it was the same story everywhere. And as he neared New York, the excitement seemed to grow.

Every town wanted to give him a dinner. If he had stopped to eat all those dinners and drink all those toasts, he would never have reached New York at all. Philadelphia greeted Washington with rapture. After all, they had a right to be proud of what had happened; much of it had happened right there!

Then, on April 21, Washington crossed the Delaware River to Trenton. All morning long, the rain poured down, but by noon, the air cleared. Washington prepared to cross the Delaware to the bustling little town which would forever be remembered because of the victory he had won there on that famous Christmas when things looked darkest.

He was met at the wharf by a troop of horse, and escorted to town amid the booming of cannon and the shouts of the townspeople who had come out to greet him.

The bridge over the little Assunpink Creek was covered by a triumphal arch twenty feet wide, supported by thirteen columns entwined with greens and flowers. And on it in great golden letters, Washington could read that "THE DEFENDER OF THE MOTHERS WILL PROTECT THEIR DAUGHTERS!"

At the approach to the bridge, a group of mothers and daughters stood with baskets of flowers in their hands, singing a song written just for the occasion:

> Welcome, mighty chief, once more!
> Welcome to this grateful shore!
> Now no mercenary foe
> Aims again the fatal blow,
> Aims at thee the fatal blow.
> Virgins fair and matrons grave,
> Those thy conquering arm did save,
> Build for thee triumphal bowers.
> Strew, ye fair, his way with flowers,
> Strew your hero's way with flowers.

It was not very good poetry, but it was all very beautiful. Washington was so touched that he kept a copy of the poem and cherished it all his life.

Then on to Princeton he went, where the college students came out to greet him, and on again to New Brunswick and Elizabeth Town. You can follow his route on any map. On April 23, he was ready for the grand entrance into New York City.

New York was to be the first capital of the new nation. Washington would take the oath of office there, give his Inaugural Address, and take up the duties of the Presidency. Naturally enough, New York wanted to show that it could outdo even Philadelphia in celebrations. And it did.

Just imagine the scene: a warm April day, the sun bright in the skies, a lively wind rippling the waters of the bay. The harbor was filled with ships of all kinds—little rowboats, fishing smacks, sailboats, schooners, packets, frigates, their flags fluttering in the breeze, their cannon booming forth salute after salute. Eager spectators crowded the boats.

It was noon when Washington and his party stepped into the splendid new barge that had been provided just for the occasion. It was fifty feet long; its awning was hung with red curtains; it was rowed by thirteen oarsmen, all masters of sailing vessels. Each was dressed in a handsome white and black uniform. As the barge began to move across the bay, all the cannon boomed and all the thousands of spectators on the boats and along the waterfront gave a great cheer.

Let Elias Boudinot tell the story. He was a member of Congress from New Jersey, and one of those who was with Washington all that day. When it was all over, he sat down and wrote his wife a full account of it:

> With a propitious gale, we left my beloved shore, and glided with steady motion across Newark Bay, the waters seeming to rejoice in bearing so precious a burden over its placid bosom. The distant appearance of the troops, the militia in uniform we had left behind, and their regular firings added much to our pleasure.
>
> When we drew near to the mouth of the Kills, a number of boats with a great variety of superb flags came up to us, and dropped on our wake. Soon after we opened the bay, General Knox and several gentlemen of distinction in a large barge presented themselves with splendid colors.
>
> Boat after boat, sloop after sloop, added to our little fleet, gaily dressed with every naval armament. We began to make a most elegant appearance.
>
> Before we got to Bedloe's Island, a large

sloop came with full sail on our starboard bow. . . . About twenty gentlemen and ladies rose up and with excellent and melodious voices sung an eloquent ode appropriate to the occasion, and set to the music of "God Save the King," welcoming their great Chief to the seat of government.

At the conclusion, we gave them our hats, and then they, with the surrounding boats, gave three hurrah's, which made the neighboring shores rebound with the joyful acclamation.

Soon after, another boat came under our stern, and threw in amongst us a number of copies of another ode. Immediately about a dozen gentlemen began to sing it in parts, as we passed along. Our worthy President was greatly affected with these tokens of profound respect and gratitude.

As we approached the harbor, our train increased, and the hurrahing and shouts of joy added great vivacity to this lively scene.

At this moment, a shoal of porpoises came rising above the water, and laying among the boats, as if desirous to know the cause of all this joy and gladness.

We now discovered the shores crowded with thousands of people, men, women, and children—nay, I venture to say tens of thousands. From the Battery to the place of landing, although nearly half a mile, you could see little else along the wharves, in the streets, and on board the vessels, but heads as numerous as ears of corn before the harvest.

The vessels in the harbor presented a most superb appearance, draped in all the pomp of national gaiety and elegance. A Spanish packet then lying in the harbor, in a moment, on a signal given, hoisted twenty-seven or twenty-eight different colors of all nations on every part of the rigging, and paid a compliment of thirteen guns with all her yards manned, as did another vessel in the harbor displaying colors in like manner. From the Battery, we had the like compliment of eighteen-pounders.

We soon arrived at the ferry stairs in Wall Street, where many thousands of citizens and a chosen detachment of the militia in elegant uniform, waited with all eagerness of expectation, welcomed this most excellent man to that shore which he had by his judgment and courageous perseverance regained from a powerful enemy almost against hope. We found the stairs covered with carpeting, and the rails from the water to the top of the wharf

Salute to General Washington in New York Harbor.

hung with crimson hangings.

The President, being preceded by the committee, was received by the Governor and the principal citizens in the most brilliant and affectionate manner.

He was met on the wharf by many of his old and faithful companions and fellow patriots, who had with him borne the heat and burden of the day, and who, like him, had experienced every reverse of fortune with fortitude and patience, and who now joined the universal chorus of welcome to the great deliverer (under Providence) from all their fears.

119

It was with difficulty a passage could be made by the troops through the pressing crowd, who seemed incapable of being satisfied in gazing at this man of the people. . . . The streets were lined with inhabitants as close as they could stand together, and it required all the exertions of a numerous train of city officers with their staves to make a passage for the procession.

The houses were filled with gentlemen and ladies elegantly dressed, the whole distance being about half a mile. The windows to the highest stories were illuminated by the sparkling eyes of innumerable companies of ladies, who seemed to vie with each other to show the joy on this great occasion.

A pair of the "sparkling eyes" belonged to a young girl, Eliza Quincy, who remembered that

Carpets were spread to the carriage prepared for him, but he preferred walking through the crowded streets, and was attended by Governor Clinton and many officers and gentlemen.

He frequently bowed to the multitude, and took off his hat to the ladies at the windows, who waved their handkerchiefs, threw flowers before him, and shed tears of joy and congratulation.

The whole city was one scene of triumphal rejoicing. His name in every form of decoration appeared on the fronts of the houses, and the streets through which he passed were ornamented with flags, silk banners of various colors, wreaths of flowers, and branches of evergreens. Never did anyone enjoy such a triumph as Washington.

X

Now WE come to the last act of all—the last act of this old drama called The Revolution, and the first act of an entirely new drama named The New Nation. That is the inauguration of Washington as President of the United States.

The inauguration had been set for the thirtieth of April. Early that morning, the bells of Christ's Church and of Trinity had begun to ring in the happy day. Soon all the other church bells took up the refrain. And New Yorkers, dressed in their Sunday best, crowded into the churches to ask the blessings of Heaven on their new government.

Precisely at noon, a military escort clattered up to the presidential house on Cherry Street. There was a cavalry company, the horses prancing impatiently to be on. There were two companies of grenadiers: one in blue with gold ornaments and white feathers in their cockade hats; the other with bright-yellow vests under bright-blue coats, and giant bearskin hats atop their sweltering heads. And best of all, there was a company of Scots Highlanders, kilts and bagpipes and all.

At twelve-thirty a handsome carriage pulled up in front of the house, and the General came out. He had dressed soberly for the occasion—a brown broadcloth suit, white silk stockings, silver buckles gleaming on his shoes, a dress sword at his side.

Off, then, to the Federal Hall, which New York City had refurbished just for this event. The new Congress was already there, waiting somewhat impatiently for the new President.

And there, too, was the Vice-President, John Adams, as nervous as a schoolboy at his first dance. He asked everyone how he should behave, what he should do, what he should say, when the President came in. As if anybody cared!

Soon the doors were flung open and the great man arrived. John Adams hastened to escort him to his seat on the little platform. There Washington sat, while all gazed upon him. Then the Chan-

George Washington takes the oath of office on the balcony
of the old City Hall in New York.

cellor of the State of New York, who was to administer the oath of office, conducted him out to
the balcony overlooking Broad Street—now Broad-
way. There the ceremony was to take place.

Our friend Eliza Quincy saw it all and remembered it:

> I was on the roof of the first house in Broad
> Street, and so near Washington that I could
> almost hear him speak. The windows and the
> roofs of the houses were crowded, and in the
> streets the throng was so dense that it seemed

as if one might literally walk on the heads of the people.

The balcony of the hall was in full view of this assembled multitude. In the center of it was placed a table with a rich covering of red velvet, and upon this on a crimson velvet cushion, lay a large and elegant Bible. This was all the paraphernalia for the august scene.

All eyes were fixed upon the balcony, where at the appointed hour Washington entered, accompanied by the Chancellor... who was to administer the oath, by John Adams, Governor Clinton, and many other distinguished men. By the great body of the people he had probably never been seen except as a military hero. The first in war was now the first in peace.

His entrance on the balcony was announced by universal shouts of joy and welcome. His appearance was most solemn and dignified. Advancing to the front of the balcony, he laid his hand on his heart, bowed several times, and then retired to an armchair near the table.

The populace appeared to understand that the scene had overcome him, and were at once hushed in profound silence. After a few moments, Washington arose and came forward.

Chancellor Livingston read the oath, according to the form prescribed by the Constitution, and Washington repeated it, resting his hand upon the table. Mr. Otis, the Secretary of the Senate, then took the Bible and raised it to the lips of Washington, who stooped and kissed the book.

At this moment, a signal was given, by raising a flag upon the cupola of the hall, for a general discharge of the artillery of the Battery. All the bells in the city rang out a peal of joy, and the assembled multitude sent forth a universal shout.

The President again bowed to the people, and then retired from a scene such as the proudest monarch never enjoyed.

Washington, and the Congress, then returned to the Senate chamber. Washington—now President —took out a manuscript, and put on his glasses, and began to read the Inaugural Address.

"The great man was agitated and embarrassed," wrote one of the Senators.

Well he might be. This wasn't just an ordinary speech. It was a speech that inaugurated not only Washington himself but a new nation.

This Inaugural Address was short—Washington was never long-winded. It was mostly a plea for understanding and help. But it made two points that are worth remembering.

Washington takes the oath of office.

First, Washington appealed to "that Almighty Being who rules the universe," that "His benediction may consecrate to the liberties and happiness of the people of the United States a government instituted by themselves for these essential purposes."

These words summed up pretty well the meaning of this Constitution and this government: a government made by the people themselves, and made for their liberty and their happiness. This was the first time in history that anything like that had happened, that people had set up their own government, and for these purposes.

The second point fitted the history of the new nation into the history of the world. Washington said,

> The preservation of the sacred fire of liberty and the destiny of the republican model of government, are justly considered, perhaps, as *deeply*, as *finally*, staked on the experiments intrusted to the hands of the American people.

It took vision to see this—and boldness to say it—that the future of liberty and of republicanism depended on this nation, still so new, so small, so weak, so untried by history. Washington had both courage and vision, and what he said proved true. It is still true today.